WILD WILD WORLD

SNAILS

by Liza Jacobs

BLACKBIRCH® PRESS

THOMSON
GALE

San Diego • Detroit • New York • San Francisco • Cleveland • New Haven, Conn. • Waterville, Maine • London • Munich

THOMSON

GALE

For more information, contact
The Gale Group, Inc.
27500 Drake Rd.
Farmington Hills, MI 48331-3535
Or you can visit our Internet site at http://www.gale.com

Photographs © 1993 by Chang Yi-Wen

Cover photograph © Corbis

© 1993 by Chin-Chin Publications Ltd.

No. 274-1, Sec.1 Ho-Ping E. Rd., Taipei, Taiwan, R.O.C.
Tel: 886-2-2363-3486 Fax: 886-2-2363-6081

LIBRARY OF CONGRESS CATALOGING-IN-PUBLICATION DATA

Jacobs, Liza.
  Snails / by Liza Jacobs.
    v. cm. -- (Wild wild world)
  Includes bibliographical references.
  Contents: Many kinds of snails -- Mating -- Hiding from danger.
  ISBN 1-4103-0034-X (hardback : alk. paper)
  1. Snails--Juvenile literature. [1. Snails.] I. Title. II. Series.

  QL430.4.J3 2003
  594'.38--dc21

                                                    2003001492

Printed in Taiwan
10 9 8 7 6 5 4 3 2 1

Table of Contents

About Snails

There are more than 50,000 kinds of snails. They live all over the world. Some snails live on the land and others live in the water. A snail is a mollusk, which is a soft-bodied animal that often has a hard shell.

Other mollusks include clams, oysters, slugs, and squid. Some snails are as small as the head of a pin. Others grow to 2 feet in length!

Snail shells are found in many colors and patterns. Some are round and some are cone-shaped. A snail's hard shell grows in the shape of a spiral. As the snail grows, the spiral gets bigger and bigger.

The Snail Body

The flat, bottom part of a snail's body that can come out of its shell is called the foot. A snail's head is actually at one end of its foot!

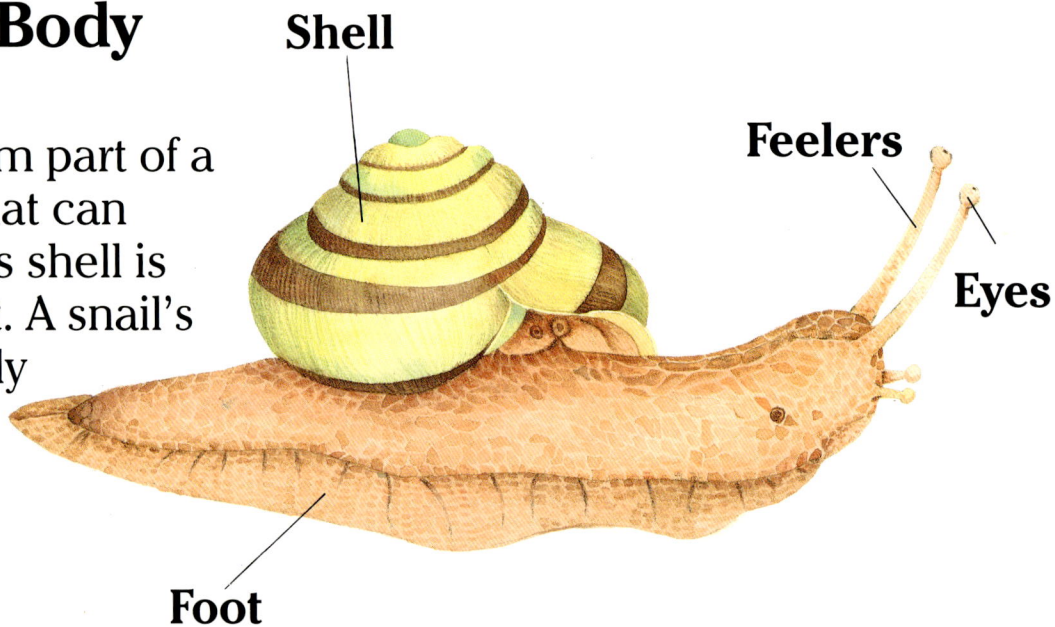

Shell

Feelers

Eyes

Foot

On their heads, snails have feelers, eyes, and a mouth. They do not have ears. Land snails have two sets of feelers, with eyes at the tips of the long ones. Some water snails have one pair of feelers and the eyes are toward the bottom of the stalks. A snail's feelers help the animal sense its way around.

The part of a snail's body that has its heart, liver, stomach, and other organs stays inside the shell.

7

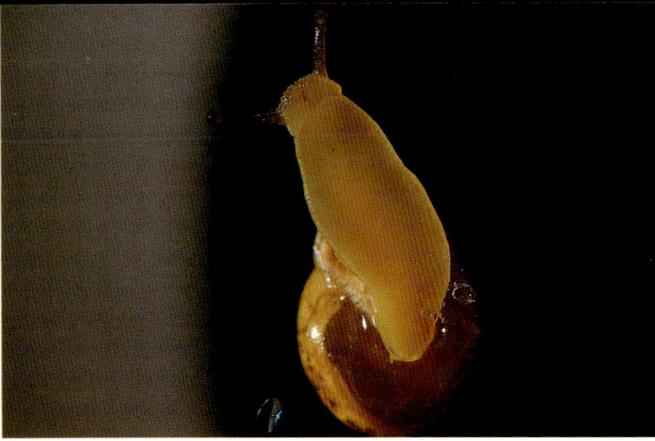

Slimy Climbing

A snail slides along by rippling the muscles in its foot.
It leaves a trail of slimy mucus behind it. The mucus
creates a kind of track for the snail to follow.

Snails move very slowly. Most travel less than 3 inches
a minute! To climb up something thin, such as a vine
or stem, a snail wraps its foot around it to keep from
falling off.

Snails can climb straight up and down. They can even climb upside down, letting the weight of their shell hang below.

Flexible Bodies

Snails have no bones! Their flexible bodies stretch easily. This helps a snail make a kind of bridge with its body to climb across any small open gap. It's the snail version of jumping!

Snail Enemies

A snail's shell protects it from animals that might otherwise eat it. But there are still many creatures that are able to get at snails in their shells.

Fish, crabs, birds, frogs, snakes, lizards, skunks, and raccoons all eat snails. Beetles can crack right through a snail shell.

Some young fireflies shoot poison into a snail's shell that turns the snail's body into liquid. Then the firefly sucks up its meal! People eat snails, too.

Eating

Land snails mainly eat leaves, buds, and vegetables. Many snails that live in the water eat water plants and some also eat animals such as clams and oysters. A close-up of the head (above) shows a snail's small, crescent-shaped mouth under the short feelers. Snails have a long, flat tongue called a radula. The radula has rows of tiny sharp teeth on it. Snails shred their food before eating it by rubbing their sharp tongues back and forth on a leaf or vegetable. When a snail poops, the waste is passed through an opening near the front edge of the shell.

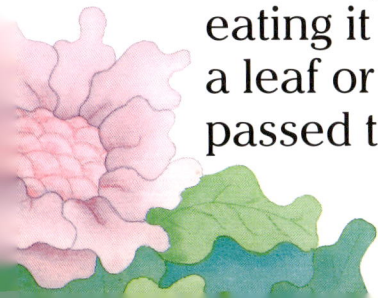

15

Mating

Water snails are usually either male or female. But most land snails have both male and female body parts. They need to mate in order to make baby snails. They lay their rubbery eggs within about a month after mating. Some snails lay their eggs in the dirt. Some attach them to leaves or stems. Other snails lay eggs under rocks or logs.

Baby
Snails

When it is time to hatch, baby land snails
push out of their eggs. They look like tiny adults, but their
shells are paper-thin. You can see right through the shell! The
first thing a baby snail eats is its eggshell. Then it begins
munching on the nearest leaves or flowers it can find.

Food to Grow

Young snails need to eat a lot of food to help them grow. The more food a snail eats, the faster it grows. And as its soft body grows, so does its shell.

Staying Moist

Snails hide in their shells to protect themselves from danger. They also go inside to keep from drying out.

Snails need to stay moist in order to survive. When the weather gets too hot or dry, a snail pulls its body inside and seals the opening of the shell with mucus. Snails can stay like this for days, and even months. They often spend winters sealed in their cozy shells.

This survival skill is one reason these interesting creatures have roamed the earth for thousands of years.

For More Information

Murray, Peter. *Snails.* Mankato, MN:
Child's World, 1998.

Pascoe, Elaine. *Snails and Slugs (Nature Close-up).* San Diego, CA:
Blackbirch Press, 1999.

Glossary

mollusk a soft-bodied animal that usually has a hard shell

radula a snail's long, flat tongue